TOKOLOSHI

In this book you will meet Vugiswe, the Zulu boy, and sit with him under the wait-a-minute tree on the African plain listening to the wonderful stories which his mother, First Woman, has to tell about Hare and Crocodile, about Lion Cub and Hyena, about Fire and Water – and about Tokoloshi himself, who is a very powerful imp even though he *is* only as long as your pointing finger and as dark as a moonless night. You will find out why Ape has no tail, why Mosquito buzzes so angrily and why Elephant ... but it would be a pity to spoil the stories by telling you too much about them. They are simple but enthralling, for they contain many secrets of Nkulunkulu's creation.

TOKOLOSHI

AFRICAN FOLK-TALES
ADAPTED AND RE-TOLD BY

Diana Pitcher

ILLUSTRATED BY
Meg Rutherford

Celestial Arts
A Dawne-Leigh Book
Millbrae, California

PRONUNCIATION

VOWELS

a   as in English *bark*

e   as in English *bed*

e   as in English *please*

o   as in English *or* or *law*

u   as in English *pool* or *rule*

CONSONANTS

As in English but g as in *gone*.

DOUBLE AND TREBLE CONSONANTS

dh   the s sound in *measure*

ndhl   is pronounced as three distinct sounds n − dh − l, e.g. Ndhlovu.

SYLLABLES

n and m are often syllables in themselves, e.g.

Nkulunkulu	n-ku-lu-n-ku-lu
Nvelingange	n-ve-lin-gan-ge
Nbelingane	n-be-lin-ga-ne

The accent or stress in all proper names in these tales falls on the penultimate syllable.

Copyright © 1980, 1981 by Diana Pitcher
Originally published in Great Britain in 1980
by Fudge & Company Limited

Dawne-Leigh Publications
231 Adrian Road
Millbrae, California 94030

First U.S. Edition, June 1981
Manufactured in the United States of America

Library of Congress Cataloging in Publication Data

Pitcher, Diana.
   Tokoloshi: African folk-tales.

   SUMMARY: Presents adaptions and retellings of 17 African folk tales, most of which are Bantu tales of southern and central Africa set against a background of Zulu family life and customs.
   1. Tales, African.   [1. Folklore—Africa]   I. Rutherford, Meg.
II. Title.
PZ7.P642To 1981   [398.2]   80-28470
ISBN 0-89742-049-7

CONTENTS

AUTHOR'S NOTE

The number of different ethnic groups in Africa makes it impossible to speak of 'African tales' as a single entity. I have chosen most of my stories therefore from those Bantu tales of southern and central Africa which make a homogeneous group and have set them against a background of Zulu family life and custom using Zulu names. I have turned to west and east Africa only where the story can be fitted into this framework. Two ideas, however, are common to all Africa south of the Sahara, except Ethiopia. Hare is always the villain, his behaviour ranging from mischievous spite to down-right malicious evil. There is universal mention of a sacred grove or pool invariably associated with a changeling child or a visitation of a supernatural creature. Moya and her Manyeleti is one version of this story.

FIRST MAN AND FIRST WOMAN

Nkulunkulu had just made the earth. There were great mountains and huge rocks and wait-a-minute thorn trees and green grass and a deep, dark pool; so deep that its waters were black; too deep even to show the colour of the sky; too deep even for Sun to pierce it with his light. At the bottom of the pool lay two serpents. The larger one was as thick as a man's body and he lay in as many coils as you have fingers and toes, each coil a little smaller than the last; and above them all lay his flat head and beady eyes and darting tongue. Next to him lay a smaller serpent, her body slimmer, her colour a little lighter, her coils numbering only the fingers on your hands, her head flatter, her eyes shinier, her forked tongue flickering more gently.

It was not only dark at the bottom of the pool – it was cold and silent; so cold that even Serpent shivered, so silent that not even Wind or Thunder could be heard when storms raged.

Then, one day, Lightning pierced the water. His great flash shot to the bottom of the pool and the waters parted for a moment and Serpent saw the world above; saw the yellow undertail of Bulbul as he drank the nectar of the red aloe; saw the large toes of Lily-trotter as she walked daintily across the leaves on top of the pool; saw the brilliant, green tips to the brown wings of Hooded Kingfisher as he dipped down to catch a small silver fish in his beak; saw the long, soft, grey tail of Mouse-bird as she clambered up the gnarled trunk of a tree; saw the scarlet breast of Sunbird and the black and orange patterns on the broad tail of Widow-bird; saw the curved, yellow beak of Hornbill; saw the striped head of Barbet and the long, crimson tail of Fly-catcher; saw the flashing red of Bee-eater as he landed on Kori-Bustard's back and the red cheeks and blue breasts of the weaver-finches building their great family nest, a nest to hold a hundred birds, in the fork of the wait-a-minute tree; and saw, just as the waters started to close again, the pale green eggs, veined with black, of ...

The waters closed over his head and Lightning drew back into the sky. Serpent's eyes blinked in the dark and he lay thinking in amazement of the beauty that lay in the world above his watery home. A quiver ran right through his body.

'Wife,' he said to the smaller serpent coiled up at his side. 'I have seen the world which Nkulunkulu has made. It is more beautiful than I can ever tell you. I cannot stay here in the darkness any longer. I must go up

and see the earth with its trees and birds, its colours and shapes, with its light and warmth.'

'How can you live on the earth?' answered the smaller serpent. 'Will you crawl on your belly while the birds of the air fly above you in the blue sky and scorn you for being so low?'

'I will not crawl on my belly,' said Serpent, 'I will walk. Come.'

Very slowly the serpents uncoiled themselves and, close together, they began to rise through the murky waters. Serpent felt a tremor run through his tail. He flicked it and felt it split, split into two separate, separate, … not two separate tails but two legs with feet on them and five toes on each foot. He kicked his legs and rose a little faster towards the surface of the water. A strange, prickling feeling ran round his neck and his arms began to grow, each with a strong hand at the end with four strong fingers and a thumb. He beat his new arms in the water and rose yet faster. His head was growing round and full and when the serpents reached the top of the pool and broke through the leaves of the water lilies they were no longer two serpents but a man and a woman.

He looked at his wife. Her round head was covered with little tight black curls, her soft brown eyes were excited as she looked about her at the beautiful earth, her shapely body was shiny brown and her long legs were firm and smooth. He knew that First Woman was the most beautiful, the most gentle, the most wise woman that Nkulunkulu would ever make.

She looked at her husband. His broad head was covered with tight black curls, his brown eyes were fearless as he looked about him at the wonderful earth, his arms and legs were strong. She knew that First Man was the cleverest, bravest man that Nkulunkulu would ever make.

'Come,' he said, taking her hand, 'let us look at this earth, these trees and stones, at these birds which flit and swoop about in the blue sky, at the grass which is soft beneath our feet. Let us warm ourselves in Sun's heat and then you shall make me a round hut with one door, and you shall cut the long grass and thatch the roof and I shall go out and hunt a young antelope and you shall make me a meal and we shall eat at the door of the hut and watch Sun sink behind the mountains and we shall sleep in the hut when darkness falls. Never again shall we live beneath the waters.'

First Man and First Woman walked across the grassy banks of the pool towards the plains.

TOKOLOSHI

First Woman was singing gaily to herself as she hoed the weeds between the rows of maize plants. The ears were growing fat and the tassels on them shone green and gold in the sunlight. Soon the cobs would be ready to pick and she would dry some of them to use during the winter months, and some she would grind into coarse yellow meal from which she would make porridge for First Man and, best of all, some she would roast in the glowing embers until the grains were crispy brown and could be eaten from the cob.

She put down the hoe for a moment and stretched her back, feeling the warmth of Sun on her skin. She stood very still and in that moment she heard a whisper in her right ear. 'Go out and seek the calabash row,' it whispered. 'Go out and seek the calabash row.'

First Woman put down the hoe and set out, away from the hut, across the plain, towards the three wait-a-minute trees growing in a straight row at the end of the deep pool. Under the trees were three calabashes, upside down, standing in a straight row. What, she thought, could this mean? They were not her calabashes. Who had put them here? Why were they upside down? First Woman was afraid. Whose voice had whispered to her as she hoed in the fields?

'Pick up the calabash.' The whisper came again in her right ear. 'Pick up the calabash.'

The air was very still. No breeze blew to ruffle the grass or shake the leaves; no bird sang. 'Pick up the calabash.' She bent down and turned over the first gourd. There was nothing there.

'Pick up the calabash.'

She bent down and turned over the second gourd. There was nothing there.

'Pick up the calabash.'

Trembling with fear she bent down and picked up the last gourd. A black shadow flitted from under it and she felt a touch, as soft as a feather, on her right shoulder. Out of the corner of her eye she saw, sitting against her neck, a small black imp, as long as your pointing finger and as dark as a moonless night. She did not turn her head or try to look at him directly. Who knows, perhaps he did not wish to be seen.

'First Woman, you have saved me from dying under the calabash,' the whisper continued. 'You are brave and good. I shall reward you. Follow me.'

The shadow flitted before her. Sometimes she could see him. Sometimes he disappeared under a stone. Sometimes he became part of the leaves of a tree. Then he appeared again, as long as your pointing finger and as dark as a moonless night. Scarcely daring to breathe she followed the imp, down the side of the kranz where Scorpion lives, over the mound where Hare frolics at night, until at length she came to a single rock on which was perched a smaller rock, shining grey in the sun.

The shadow flitted back to her shoulder.

'Push the small rock off the large rock.' The whisper was in her ear again. 'Push the small rock off the large rock.'

First Woman looked up at the small rock. It was smaller than the large one, but it was still a very heavy rock. If only First Man were here to help her.

She clambered up over the large rock, grazing her knees and toes as she did so, and heaved with all her might at the smaller one. At first it did not move.

'Push,' whispered the voice, 'push.'

Again she heaved at the rock, perched so high, and suddenly she felt it move, a little, a little more, and then a little more. She gave one last push and over toppled the rock with a great crash. Below it she saw a deep, dark cave and in the cave something was moving. She jumped back on to the grass and waited.

Out of the cave stepped first a great bull with broad, heavy shoulders and a great hump on his neck and a fierce glint in his eye. Then came a cow and three dainty heifers, picking their leaf-brown way down the rock on to the green grass which they started to graze. There followed an impudent billy-goat, his beard as grey as the rock from which he had come, and behind him three pretty little nanny-goats, their hooves picking the path easily over the face of the rock.

'Drive home your herd, First Woman,' whispered the voice in her ear. 'The cow will give calves and the calves will give more calves. They will grow into cows to give milk which you may drink, and the bull-calves will grow into oxen to draw your plough and to give meat when the hunting is bad. Take care of the goats. When the cows run dry the goats will give milk and the flesh of the goats will roast in your fire and fill your bellies when the antelopes leave the plains. Go in peace, First Woman,' and the black sprite disappeared.

First Woman drove the herd home and waited for First Man to come back from the hunt.

You can imagine his amazement when he returned to find three gourds of milk under the wait-a-minute tree and a pot full of delicious goat meat stewing over the fire. His amazement was even greater when First Woman told her story.

11

'You have talked with Tokoloshi,' he said. 'He is a great and powerful spirit even though he *is* only as big as your pointing finger and as dark as a moonless night.'

That is how First Man and First Woman came to keep flocks and herds.

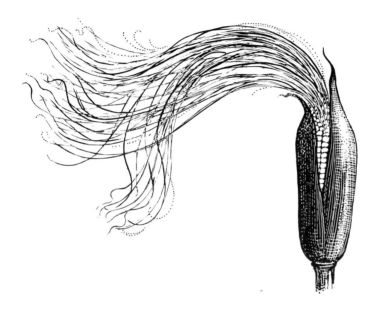

THE CALABASH CHILD

First Woman had worked very hard. There is much to do when there is no-one to help. First Man was either out hunting or sitting in the sun outside the door of his hut — for everyone knows that the work of hoeing and weeding and cooking and cleaning is the work of women and children. So First Woman cleaned the hut and ground the maize in between two flat stones and cooked the porridge and milked the cows and set the milk in calabashes under the shade of the trees where it turned sour and formed delicious, thick amasi, and hoed the fields and tended the goats. And at the end of the day she was very tired. Now if First Woman could have a child there would be someone to help her.

She stopped grinding the maize and sat up, stretched her stiff shoulders and raised her head up to Sun so that his warmth could fall upon her. She would like to have a boy-child. While he was young he could help with the herds, that was the work she found hardest, and when he grew older he would marry a wife who would have more children who would help her in her daily work. Yes, she would like to have a strong, brown baby boy who would grow up to be a fearless hunter like First Man.

She sat staring at the far distant mountains. The world was very beautiful at this time of the year. The green grass was just beginning to show above the brown earth; the trees were showing pale, green leaves; Barbet, with his striped head, was darting hither and thither; and hundreds of the blue-breasted weaver-finches, busily building their family house in the wait-a-minute tree at the head of the pool, were skimming through the sky making little blue flashes of air whenever Sun caught them in one of his rays.

She sighed and heard the sigh returned in her ear.

'Plant the calabash seeds,' whispered the sigh into her right ear. 'Plant the calabash seeds.'

First Woman knew where that whisper came from. She knew, without looking, that on her shoulder sat Tokoloshi, as big as your pointing finger and as dark as a moonless night, and she knew no-one ever disobeyed Tokoloshi.

She left off grinding the meal, went into the hut and took one gourd from inside the thatch where she had stored it to keep it fresh. She cut it open and scooped out the seeds. Going behind the hut she carefully dug over a small patch of ground and planted the seeds in two straight rows. Then she took the empty shells down to the pool and filled them with

water, came back, and watered the ground. She looked out of the corner of her eye at her right shoulder but Tokoloshi had disappeared. She started to grind the maize again.

When First Woman woke up next morning she saw that the seeds had started to grow. The plants were as high above the ground as the distance from your little finger to your thumb when you stretch your fingers wide. By evening the plants reached her shoulders and on one plant was one flower. When Sun rose on the second morning the flower was wide open. When Sun rose on the third morning the flower had turned into a big, ripe gourd. Before she went to sleep First Woman cut the gourd from the vine and put it into the thatch of her hut to keep it from Sun's heat so that it should dry slowly and not split its skin.

When Sun rose on the fourth morning First Woman went out to hoe her fields. She was really very tired today. Although the clouds had come into the sky every afternoon the rains had not come and the ground was hard and dry. The maize plants were yellow and she was afraid they might not grow strong enough to bear cobs. The hoeing was difficult. It was strange how weeds continued to grow even when the plants died.

She made her way back to the hut when Sun was directly above her — and stood still in astonishment. The floor had been swept. The calabash shells were full of milk and waited only to be put out in the shade. The old maize cobs had been stacked neatly waiting to be used for the evening fire. The grain had been carefully ground into coarse, yellow meal. She sat down in the sunshine outside the doorway and waited for First Man to return. It was good to sit still and rest awhile.

As Sun set over the mountains First Man returned across the plains. He saw his wife seated outside the hut and realised she was fast asleep. At first he was very angry. If First Woman were sleeping it meant his dinner would not be ready. He was also worried. He had seen no antelope today. Even Springbok had disappeared. It was because the water holes were dry and the animals were wandering away from the plains in search of water to drink.

He strode up to the hut and was just about to shake First Woman roughly when he caught the delicious smell of stewing meat and roasting maize and he saw that Fire was burning and the cooking pot was full and the cobs were browning in the glowing embers.

First Woman heard him gasp in surprise and roused herself from sleep.

'How have you cleaned the hut and cooked the dinner even as you slept?' asked First Man.

First Woman told him what had happened, how she had planted the gourd seed and picked the calabash and hidden it in the thatch; how she had grown tired in the fields and come home to find all the work done and the dinner cooking.

First Man sat still for a long time before he spoke. 'Tokoloshi,' he said at last, 'is a powerful spirit even if he *is* only as long as your pointing finger.'

'And as dark as a moonless night,' added First Woman.

'Where did you hide the gourd?' asked First Man.

'In the thatch, up there,' and First Woman pointed to the exact place.

First Man stretched up his arms and pulled the thatch apart. Sitting there was a small brown boy, his skin shiny, his teeth white, his eyes big and brown, his limbs smooth and strong, his smile friendly.

'Tokoloshi has sent you a son,' said First Man.

'We will call him Vugiswe,' said First Woman, 'Vugiswe – he who will waken our people and make them great,' and she gathered the little boy up in her arms and cradled him that he might sleep comfortably and safely.

4

RAINBOW

Still the rains did not come. The maize plants had shrivelled up and were quite dead. The grass was brown and hard and the cattle could not eat it. The cows were so thin that their ribs were sticking through their skins; they could give no milk and their calves cried daily. Soon, if it did not rain, the calves would die.

First Man came back from the hunt empty-handed. No game was left on the plain. There was no meat to be had. The goats were too thin for eating. There was no maize. If it did not rain soon there would be no food to eat and First Man would die.

Vugiswe lay beside the hut. He was too tired to move. First Woman had spent all day looking for bark or berries that she could boil in a soup for him but Sun had shrivelled up everything that grew and there was no food left. If it did not rain soon Vugiswe would die.

First Woman made her way down to the pool. The trees on the edge bore no leaves. There was no sign of Bulbul or Mouse-bird or Kingfisher. There was no water in the pool. She could see deep down to the very bottom which was caked and cracked, burning in Sun's rays. There was no water to drink. If it did not rain soon First Woman would die.

Sun shone brightly each day. He rose in a cloudless sky every morning. The black clouds gathered round him every afternoon and floated away over the mountains every evening and still there was no rain. First Man grew thin and tired. First Woman grew thin and weary. Vugiswe grew too weak even to ask for food.

'Nkulunkulu,' cried First Woman one evening. 'Nkulunkulu, the beautiful world you made is dying. The grass does not grow, the herds cannot graze, the birds no longer sing. Nkulunkulu have pity on your world, have pity on your people.' All night she stood outside her hut, her arms raised to the mountains where she was sure Nkulunkulu lived, her voice growing weaker and weaker as she kept repeating, 'Nkulunkulu have pity on your world, have pity on your people.'

Up in the mountains Nkulunkulu heard her voice and his heart grew gentle. He raised his eyes to the sky and called upon his father, Nvelingange, the great, powerful Nvelingange, who lives with his feet upon the clouds and his head above the blue.

'Father,' he begged, 'you let me make the earth, now you are destroying it. Send rain, my Father, or my people will die.'

Nvelingange heard his son and his heart grew sad for Nkulunkulu's earth.

Next morning Sun did not rise. The whole sky was covered with black clouds, so thick that Nkulunkulu could not see Nvelingange's feet resting on them. Lower and lower drifted the clouds until even the mountains were hidden and Nkulunkulu could not see through them to the plains. Nvelingange caught Lightning by the tail and hurled him through the black cloud-mass. Lightning sizzled between the clouds and struck the rocks, from which First Woman's herds had come, with a blinding light. Thunder roared in reply and as his voice echoed across the plain the rain began to fall. Great heavy drops of water began to beat holes in the dry earth, beat branches off the dry trees, beat the finches' old nest to the ground, beat on the thatch of First Woman's hut trying to make holes in it – but First Woman was the best thatcher in the world and the rain could not enter her hut.

Great rivers of rain swept down from the mountains and across the plain, filling the water holes, filling First Woman's pool, filling the empty roots of the trees and the grass. All day the rain beat upon the earth while First Man and First Woman and Vugiswe watched from the door of their hut, for never had they seen the clouds so dark, or Lightning so bright; never had they heard Thunder so loud; never had they heard so much water rushing across the earth.

Then, as night approached, the drops of rain became smaller, falling more gently. The clouds grew lighter and moved aside to show little patches of pale blue sky.

A rich smell came from the earth, the smell of new grass growing, of new leaves bursting from new buds. A cloud of steam rose above the great pool, now full of dark, cold water. Kingfisher dipped down and caught a silver fish.

First Woman looked out of the hut and a glorious sight met her eyes – a sight even more wonderful than that First Man saw when he was a serpent looking through the water at the birds of the air.

Right across the sky, stretched in a great arc from the mountains to the plain, was a band of colours, red, yellow, blue, green, orange. There was one last, deep clap of thunder and in it First Woman heard Nvelingange's voice, the only time, ever, ever, ever, that any one has heard Nvelingange. 'Look upon the rainbow, O woman,' said the voice. 'It is my sign that never again will I withhold the rain so that men cry for food while the earth dies. Look upon the rainbow. It is my pledge.'

And First Woman knew that she need never fear again. However dry it might get, however long the rains took to come, never again would Nvelingange threaten the world with death. His rainbow was his pledge and Nvelingange always kept his word.

5

DOG

The winter was the coldest First Man could remember. The clouds, which usually covered the sky only in summer, had settled on the mountains, hiding the peaks for many days, and when they lifted and let Sun shine through again there was a glittering white cape on the mountain tops. Wind, who usually blew warmly from the plain to the mountains, changed her direction and came bustling and flurrying from the mountains to the plain. She was cold, colder even than the water had been at the bottom of the pool where First Man had lived when he was a serpent.

First Woman made cloaks of antelope skins for First Man and for Vugiswe and then one for herself, to try to keep out the cold, but even so they shivered whenever they left the hut.

It was so cold that even the animals of the plain began to wander further afield and soon there was little game to be seen anywhere. Only Hyena and Dog were left and they were both nearly starving. Hyena is used to following Lion and eating what Lion leaves, and Dog had always followed Hyena. Now Lion had gone and neither Hyena nor Dog could find any game small enough to attack for themselves. Each day they grew colder and hungrier until at last Hyena said, 'Let us leave the plain as Lion has done. Let us follow Lion for I am dying of hunger.' Together they set out.

Suddenly Dog stopped. He could smell meat, cooking meat, and the saliva dribbled from his mouth and his stomach rumbled. He knew where the smell came from. It came from First Woman's cooking pot. He also knew First Woman had no love for Hyena who often attacked the young calves of the herd or stole the fat young pullets as they scratched for food in the dusty earth. Dog knew that First Woman hated them; but he also knew that unless he ate soon he would die.

'Let us go to First Woman's hut, Hyena,' he said. 'Surely she will give us food.'

'Are you mad?' answered Hyena. 'Do you not know First Woman has Fire? Fire burns. It burns the ground around you, it burns the grass and the trees, it burns your paws, it singes the hair off your skin. I would rather die than approach Fire.' And Hyena jogged on.

Dog raised his nose and smelled the meat again. He would risk Fire. Settling low on his belly, his front legs bent, his haunches only a little higher than his shoulders, he squirmed his way towards the smell of meat.

Now he could see First Man and First Woman and Vugiswe sitting round the orange flames which licked at the wood and ate it up, which cast eerie, flickering shadows across the grass towards Dog himself. It was true Fire would burn if it caught him, but if he could get just a little closer, not too close, but just a little closer, he would feel its warmth and there was just a chance that First Man or First Woman might toss aside a bone when they had eaten the meat off it.

Dog dropped even lower on to the ground and wriggled a little closer. He stopped and gave a tiny growl. First Man looked up. He saw the cringing creature but took no notice. No wild creature would approach too near to Fire.

Dog took one, slow step forward. He could just feel the warmth of Fire now. If he could get a little nearer perhaps the cold, frozen stiffness would leave his body. Even if he couldn't eat he could at least be warm. Vugiswe looked up. He rather liked the look of Dog, liked his smooth brown coat, his pointed black nose; but everyone knew Dog was wild and hunted with Hyena. Vugiswe bent forward and took another piece of meat from the cooking pot.

Very, very slowly Dog took one step nearer; his tail gave one little wag. He whined. First Woman looked up. She saw Dog's thin, bony body and knew the hunger that gnawed at his stomach; she saw the trembling of his limbs and understood the cold that ate into his being. She looked into Dog's pleading eyes. They were not the eyes of a hyena or a jackal. They were eyes that told of courage, of love, of devotion.

She picked up a bone and held it out. Dog crawled nearer. Would First Woman strike him with it? Would she throw it at him? She still held the bone in her hand. He opened his mouth. She sat quite still. He took the bone. She moved that he might lie nearer the flames. She put out her hand very gently and patted his head. And Dog became man's slave.

CROCODILE AND HARE

When Wind finally hid herself again in the roots of the trees and at the bottom of the secret lake, and Sun began to shine more warmly, the white cape on the mountain tops grew smaller and smaller and from its edges little trickles of water began to make their way down the slopes. At first they picked their way round rocks, chattering over the pebbles and gurgling round the roots of trees. As they reached the bottom of the slopes they swept together into one great rush of water and made their way towards the plain taking with them Water Rat and Vole, Fish and Frog, Tadpole and Water Snake, Snail and Duck – and Crocodile. By the time River reached First Woman's hut He was broad and deep, glinting in the sunshine, bringing water for drinking and water for washing, water for cooking and water to play in.

Vugiswe was squatting on River's banks, rolling and fashioning little balls of clay into a team of oxen. He pushed out each horn, smoothed down each nose, worked up each humped back until four oxen stood, two by two, beside him on the grass. He lay back, his hands behind his head, his toes just touching the water.

From the other bank a large grey creature slid silently into the water, his long, grey snout looking uncommonly like a log of dried wood as it pushed its way through the water.

Kingfisher saw it and swooped up into a tree above Vugiswe's head, clicking his beak and shaking his wings. Vugiswe smiled at him. 'You should be diving for silver fish, little bird,' he said.

Mousebird saw the grey log and scrambled up the trunk of the tree, shaking her long grey tail at Vugiswe who laughed to see a bird behaving like a four-legged animal. He always loved watching Mousebird climbing trees.

Lilytrotter lifted one foot, saw the log approaching and, opening her wings, fled up the banks with a rush of air. 'What is worrying you, little bird that walks on the water?' asked Vugiswe drowsily, for the heat was making him sleepy.

In a flurry of red and blue the weaver-finches darted in clouds above their nest, chittering, chattering, warning.

Hare lay in the long grass and watched. *He* knew what was going to happen. *He* could have roused Vugiswe by leaping and lolloping towards him but Hare did not love his fellow creatures so he sat quite still on his haunches and waited, and waited …

The log came closer and closer. The grass shivered. The leaves of the wait-a-minute tree quivered. Crocodile opened his mouth, wider, wider – and First Woman came running across the plain.

As Crocodile's jaw closed on Vugiswe's toes his scream filled the air, rolled across the plain, echoed in the mountains, set the thorns on the tree shaking, sent the finches in clouds into the sky, and brought First Woman to his side.

As Crocodile, with a smile from eye to eye, began to drag Vugiswe down the bank First Woman picked up a real log of wood and brought it down with a resounding smack on the long, grey nose. Now, although Crocodile is covered with a skin so thick that First Man cannot pierce it with his spear, his nose is very soft and is very easily hurt.

As the log of wood hit him he roared with pain, let go of Vugiswe's toes and turned on First Woman opening wide his hideous jaws again to show his yellow teeth and snapping at her arms. Again and again First Woman brought down the log on Crocodile's nose while the breeze held its breath and Widow-bird hid in the grass and Vugiswe crawled up the bank and away from the water. Down came the log again, and Crocodile slid back into the water.

First Woman turned on Hare.

'You saw,' she said, 'and you did not warn,' and she gave Hare a sharp smack with the log across his nose, splitting it in two. Then, picking up Vugiswe, she hurried back to the hut to wrap his torn toes in cool banana leaves and rock him in her arms.

A little later Vugiswe lay on an antelope skin and watched First Woman grinding maize for the evening meal. She had tackled Crocodile alone. Truly, she was a wonderful woman.

To this day Hare and his children and his children's children remember First Woman too, for all Hare's family still have split noses.

LIONESS

Vugiswe had been out tracking with Dog who had shown him where to find birds and rock-rabbits and hares. He had watched Dog dig for a mole; and he had brought back a rabbit, flushed out by Dog, for his supper. He was tired now and hungry as he squatted against the hut wall and watched First Woman preparing the cobs of maize for roasting, and skinning the rabbit for this evening's stew. Dog, lying beside him, licked his foot. He looked down and noticed, as he often did, the scars which Crocodile had made on his toes.

'First Woman,' he said, 'you are a great woman. What made you so brave that you could attack Crocodile with only a log of wood in your hand?'

First Woman sat back too, comfortably.

'Come close to me and while we soak up Sun's last rays I will tell you a story.'

Vugiswe wriggled with delight. Not only could First Woman cook the most delicious food in the world, she could also tell the best stories. He leant against her and fingered the pleated antelope-hide skirt, and admired the beads round her ankles, and waited.

'Once there was a small pride of lions, small because as yet Lion had only one wife and she had only one cub. They were happy enough. Lioness had made a comfortable and safe den for her child where she could teach him daily the games that all lion-children must learn, tracking, stalking, leaping, holding. Lion was a good father and a great hunter so he found food for them daily and the pride was sleek and fat.

One day, it was when the great drought first began, Lion had had to travel far afield to find game and did not return at sundown.

The cub grew hungry and quarrelsome and Lioness grew more and more afraid. She could not leave her baby to seek Lion and if he did not return they would starve.

For five days she waited and she was weak with hunger. Twice she had caught a small rabbit for her cub but there had not been enough meat for two and her flanks were sunken and her mouth dry. When Sun set on the sixth day she drew the cub towards her and lay down to sleep.

She was disturbed by a strange smell, a musty smell. She sniffed. The smell was growing stronger. A twig crackled. Her ears pricked and her body trembled. Two glowing pinpricks of light shone through the long

grass. Now she recognised the smell – Leopard. Driven wild by hunger, for you remember that most animals left the plain during the long drought, Leopard was considering doing something he had never done before, he was considering taking a lion cub for his supper.

Lioness nosed the cub from her side and took the scruff of his neck gently in her mouth. Quietly, so quietly that not even the grass whispered with her passing, she made her way down to the river banks. Behind her she could hear Leopard grunting. Her heart began to thump in her chest. If only she were not so hungry she would be able to move more quickly. Along the bank she padded, over the fallen trees, across the rocky outcrop. Faster and faster she padded, her breath coming in little short gasps, her flanks heaving. Sick with hunger and thirst as she was she dared not stop even to drink, for Leopard's paws padded ever closer.

Lioness scrambled over three large rocks, tearing her paws on their sharp edges, and came to a cave that stood behind them. The opening was narrow, the floor sandy, the river very near. Here she could protect her child. She dropped him gently and pushed him into the cave with her forepaw. She turned to face Leopard, waiting, silent, still, her hackles rising, weakness creeping into her body.

Suddenly the plains rang with grunts and snarls. The earth shook as Leopard sprang and met the full force of Lioness's body as she hurled all her weight at him. Leopard put out his claws and ripped the skin from her flanks. She buried her teeth in his neck and he started back in pain and surprise. He crouched. She waited. He leapt. She put out her claws and tore the rippling muscles in his shoulder. He whimpered, hesitated, and with one final effort her body flew through the air and landed on his back. Her teeth sunk deeply into the flesh of his neck.

The moles trembled beneath the earth as Leopard's blood came seeping through to their holes. Widow-bird fled from the topmost branch of the tree. Leopard gave one strangled snarl and dragged himself off into the bush. Lioness lay down. She was bleeding from her flanks, the pads of her feet were torn and bruised, she had lost three claws and she was very thirsty and very tired. She turned slowly and painfully so that she filled the cave entrance – none could enter and reach her cub. She lay with her back to the entrance, her stomach facing her child.

When Lion found his cub two days later, he was eating the soft flesh of Lioness's underbelly. He was sleek and fat, safe and well.

Remember Vugiswe, you may attack Lion; you may attack Lioness; but never, never, never attack the cub.'

FIRE

First Woman was quiet for a long time. Vugiswe sat still. He was thinking of Lioness and of First Woman for he had understood the story. As long as he lived with First Woman he need never fear. Like Lioness she would protect him from all danger – until he grew up and took a wife. Then his wife would become the lioness and protect her children, they would be his children too. He was glad he belonged to First Woman.

Fire flickered. He needed more wood. Gently Vugiswe moved away from First Woman – she seemed to be dreaming with her eyes open and he did not wish to disturb her. He went over to the wait-a-minute tree and collected some more branches and came back and blew on the embers and fed the wood to Fire, one piece at a time, until the stew was bubbling again and the cobs began to brown.

After dinner, as they sat about the embers, Vugiswe heard Lion roar. He shivered and crept closer to First Woman. He was afraid of Lion. First Woman drew him towards her.

'Have no fear,' she said, 'Lion will not approach Fire. He fears Fire more than anything else on earth.'

'Where did you get Fire from, First Woman?'

'We have had enough stories for one day,' she answered. 'Tomorrow when we have cleaned the hut and weeded the fields and milked the cows you shall help me strip the grains from the maize cobs and while I grind the meal I shall tell you the story of Fire. He is a great friend, but a terrible enemy. It is as well that you should know all about him.'

Vugiswe worked hard the next morning. He swept the floor of the hut and replastered it with soft wet dung until it shone. He piled up cobs and twigs nearby for feeding to Fire when First Woman started cooking later in the day. He filled the gourds with milk and set them in the shade where the milk could slowly sour and thicken. He smacked his lips. He loved eating the thick amasi that milk turned into if it did not sour too quickly. He even helped First Woman hoe the maize patch, although that was really not boy's work. Then he settled down to stripping the cobs and waited for First Woman to begin.

'At the end of the great drought, just before the Great One sent the rain, the earth was very dry. The leaves had died and fallen from the trees into great crisp, brown piles; the sap had stopped rising and the branches were brittle and cracked. The grass was brown and hard. Rivers and water holes

were empty. The earth cried for water. One day Lightning was teasing all Nkulunkulu's creation. He zigzagged across the sky, this way and that, and Thunder chased him and roared at him. To escape Thunder he zinged down into the woods over there,' First Woman pointed to the wooded slopes of the foothills, 'and licked a dry msasa tree. Suddenly Fire shot from the tree in great flames, reaching into the sky higher than my arms can reach even when I stretch them. From tree to tree Fire rushed, eating up the branches in his crackling, smoking hunger. He ran across the grass, through the piles of leaves, across the grey rocks that split in his great heat, and leaped over the dry river beds.

Antelope and Monkey, Lizard and Ape, Hare and Elephant fled before him, thundering across the plains while First Man and I sat huddled in our hut and begged Nkulunkulu to protect us, for the earth shook with the terror of their hooves. Kingfisher left the river bed and fled, high in the sky, before the hot winds that Fire pushed ever closer to us. Gnat and Beetle, Locust and Grasshopper, unable to fly high enough or fast enough, were swallowed by Fire; Widow-bird, hampered by her long tail, was singed and dropped into the devouring flames. A cloud of smoke hid Sun from our eyes, the smell of burnt grass and burnt game filled our heads, flying black dust filled our eyes, and then, just when we thought we must surely die, Nkulunkulu sent the rain.

The earth hissed and sizzled, the black dust ran down our thatch and the walls of our hut, and the rivers flowed black water. Rain is stronger than Fire so we knew we were saved. But before Fire died First Man caught a sliver of his flame and flung it beneath the cooking pot.

We have Fire now to warm us and cook our food, but never, Vugiswe, *never* let Fire out of your sight. He is mischievous and cannot be trusted. He will lick up the grass and eat the trees, he will eat your hut itself if you give him the chance. Keep him chained to one place and he is your greatest friend.

Come now, let us put the water in the pot and have Fire heat it. When it boils I will make putu.'

Vugiswe rubbed his stomach. He loved the thick, yellow porridge, the putu, that First Woman made from the ground maize. He hoped First Man would not be late. A story *and* putu in one day. He really was very lucky to be First Woman's son.

SEA, SUN AND MOON

Vugiswe had worked very hard all morning helping First Woman. Now he was free, free to make clay oxen, or walk along River's banks, (keeping a sharp eye on Crocodile), or, well, anything. Perhaps he would just lie down for a few minutes and let Sun shine on him and the breeze blow over him. He stretched out under the wait-a-minute tree, his hands clasped behind his head. He closed his eyes against the bright light and smiled to himself with joy as he felt the warmth on his skin, and in his bones, and the pleasant fulness of his stomach. This was a wonderful world in which he lived. Everything was very quiet for a moment, then he heard Honey-bird calling, 'Hon-eee, hon-ee'. He wondered who had taught Honey-bird to call her name and how it was she always found the nests of wild bees. There were so many things he did not know yet. He must ask First Woman. He was growing up and soon he would be going out with his father every day and there would be no time to hear any more stories. Come to think of it, why did Sun and Moon live in the sky? And how did they get there?

First Woman would be stripping cobs now and this was always a good time for stories, before she actually started preparing the food in the cooking pots. He squinted up at the sky to see exactly where Sun was. Yes, there would be time for a story before Sun hid behind the mountains, which was the time First Woman always became so busy.

Vugiswe scrambled to his feet and made his way back to the hut.

'Yes,' said First Woman. 'I can tell you why Sun and Moon live in the sky *and* how they got there. Come, sit by me and stack the cobs while I strip them and you shall hear the story.'

Vugiswe smiled to himself. He believed First Woman liked telling stories as much as he liked listening to them.

'When Nkulunkulu first made the earth he divided it into three kraals. Sun lived in one. Moon lived in one and Water lived in one. Round each kraal was a strong stockade made of scrub and thorn trees, rocks and sand.

Sun and Moon were great friends and both loved Water and often visited her in her kraal where they were always welcomed and well entertained. But Water never visited Sun or Moon.

One day Moon said to Sun, "We visit Water regularly. Why does Water never visit us? Do you think she feels too superior, feels that our kraals are not fit for her to visit?"

At first Sun laughed at such an idea but day after day Moon muttered and grumbled until Sun, too, began to wonder why Water always remained at home.

Then, one hot summer's day, Moon said to Sun, "You must insist on Water visiting us. You must accept no excuses this time. Water is insulting us by her refusal."

So Sun insisted. When Water finally said she could not come because neither Sun's nor Moon's kraal was big enough, not even if they were joined together to make one kraal, Sun replied angrily, "There is plenty of room. You will visit us at noon tomorrow." Water smiled a little, sad smile and accepted the invitation, which was really more like a command.

At noon next day Water began to trickle in through Sun's stockade, a little trickle at first, just a trickle. "See," said Sun, "there is plenty of room." The trickle continued; the hole in the stockade grew bigger; Water continued to visit. By evening the trickle had become a rush and with Water had come weeds and fish and water plants. Sun frowned. His kraal was nearly covered by now and Water had started to flow through Moon's stockade, throwing up ripples as high as a man's head, bringing Shark, who eats man's flesh, and Whale, who blows fountains through a hole in his head. Deep blue was Water now, as blue as the sky above, and the large ripples, which First Man calls waves, were tipped with white froth.

Sun climbed on to the roof of his hut, Moon clambered up on to hers. Water continued to flow. Finally Sun fled from her and leaped up into the sky, shaking his fist at Moon.

Now Moon was in trouble, too. If she stayed where she was she would drown. If she leaped into the sky to join Sun he might well, in his anger, hurl her back, for she knew it was her fault that Sun had insisted on Water's visit. Water rose higher and higher. With a cry of fury Sun sank down behind the mountains in the west. With a cry of relief Moon leaped up into the sky in the east. Water covered the two compounds and Sea was born.'

From that day to this Moon keeps as far as she can from Sun in the sky — they have never dared to come back to earth — and Sea hurls herself at the sand and rocks and dunes that are all that is left of Sun's and Moon's beautiful kraals.'

'Where is Sea?' asked Vugiswe.

'Many days' journey from here. Soon, when you are a little older, First Man will take you there. It is a great sight.'

Vugiswe did not know if he really wanted to grow older. It would be very exciting to visit Sea, but he would miss First Woman's splendid stories.

MOSQUITO

Slap! Vugiswe brought his hand down hard on his knee. Mosquito buzzed lazily. Slap! Vugiswe slapped his own cheek hard, but he missed again and Mosquito buzzed off.

'Hush,' whispered First Woman, 'you will wake First Man.'

'If only Mosquito did not buzz so loudly,' said Vugiswe quietly. 'He makes so much noise.'

'But Mosquito cannot help buzzing. He is cursed and his buzz *is* his curse.'

Vugiswe sat up.

'Oh no, no stories now. Go to sleep and I will tell you about Mosquito in the morning.'

When First Man had eaten and the cooking pots had been scoured First Woman began.

'We were coming home from gathering bark in the foothills (First Man was going to make some medicine) and there, round the bend of the river, tucked in among some rocks, was a mango tree so full of ripe fruit that even now my mouth waters to think of it. We came back to the hut, got ready a bag in which to carry the fruit and decided to set out early the next morning.

First Man climbed the tree and settled himself in the fork of a branch when, sting! Mosquito bit him on the cheek. First Man jerked back, without stopping to think, and in doing so caused a laden branch to shake, and down came as many ripe mangoes as you have toes, right above my head.

I leaped aside for a large ripe mango can do much damage when it falls from a high branch. As I touched the earth again I felt Rat slither away from under my feet.

Terrified by the commotion Rat shot up the trunk of a nearby tree and collided with Monkey who was perched high up among the smaller, leafy branches, eating a banana.

Monkey hates Rat and with an angry chattering and tongue clicking he threw his half-eaten banana down and fled higher up the tree, caught hold of a creeper and swung himself across the gap between his tree and the next. Perhaps because he was frightened, perhaps because his hands were wet with banana, Monkey slipped and crashed down on to a great nest of red ants.

Helter skelter ran the ants, here, there and everywhere, and straight into Brown Hen's nest. Brown Hen was sitting on a clutch of eggs dreaming of the yellow chickens she would soon have, when she felt the ants swarm through her feathers. With a loud cackle she scrambled off her nest and her toes, in her panic, broke the eggs.

Brown Hen could not be comforted. Her first clutch of eggs, and there would be no chickens! Her sorrow was pitiful to see. Cockerel stroked her wings and head gently, and crowed little, tiny crows, but Hen's heart was broken. All afternoon she wept, and all night and the following morning Cockerel was so busy comforting Hen that he forgot to crow.

You know, of course, it is Cockerel's task to wake Sun every morning. Cockerel did not crow so Sun did not wake and the sky remained dark. I had to work by Fire's light in the hut but it is hard to go out and milk the cows in the dark. Their udders were full and they lowed piteously.

The next day Cockerel crowed – late, but he did crow and Sun rose in the east and daylight came.

"Why was I not wakened yesterday?" demanded Sun.

"I was comforting Hen and in our sorrow I forgot," answered Cockerel humbly.

"Why was Hen in need of comfort?" demanded Sun.

"Because in my fear of the ants I had trampled my clutch of eggs," answered Brown Hen sorrowfully.

"Why were the ants terrifying Hen?" demanded Sun.

"Because Monkey had landed in our nest and we were in a great panic," answered all the ants together.

"Why did Monkey break Ants' nest?" demanded Sun.

"Because I saw Rat coming up the tree at me and I tried to swing to another tree and my hands slipped," chattered Monkey furiously.

"Why was Rat climbing the tree?" demanded Sun.

"First Woman stood on my tail," answered Rat nervously.

"Why did First Woman stand on Rat's tail?" demanded Sun.

"Because I was afraid the mangoes dropped by First Man would hurt my head," I answered meekly.

"Why did First Man drop the mangoes?" demanded Sun.

"Because Mosquito bit me on the cheek," answered First Man firmly.

"Why did Mosquito bite you on the cheek?" demanded Sun.

But Mosquito refused to answer.

"All this trouble," said Sun, "of wasted mangoes, frightened rats, angry monkeys, broken nests, dead chickens AND no-one to wake me yesterday; all this because of an unexpected bite from Mosquito who now refuses to answer. In future," Sun looked straight at Mosquito as he spoke, "in future man shall always know exactly where you are for you shall buzz. No more shall you come upon man without his knowledge."

Mosquito lost his power of speech at that very moment and he has buzzed ever since.'

11

MOYA

It was the last night before Vugiswe was to leave to pay the bride price. He knew that First Man must have found a very good, hard-working girl for him, for the bride price was high – five sleek oxen, ten healthy brown cows and a young bullock. He was sitting before the fire with First Man and First Woman. The embers had burned low. The stars were very bright for Moon had not yet risen. The frogs were singing on River's banks and once Bush Baby cried softly from the trees. Vugiswe felt peaceful and contented.

First Man stirred.

'I think,' he said turning towards First Woman, 'that we should tell Vugiswe about his sister.'

'My sister!' Vugiswe sat up straight in astonishment. 'But I have no sister.'

First Woman smiled sadly.

'Yes,' she said. 'I think we should tell him.' She sat very still staring out across the plain at a small copse of trees growing on a little knoll.

'Your sister came to us long before Tokoloshi brought you. She was the gift of Wind, that is why we called her Moya. She was a very beautiful child. Her brown eyes shone. Her smile was as bright and happy as Sun after Rain. Her legs were straight and smooth, as smooth as the round pebbles River throws up on the banks.

She was a loving girl and helped me willingly with my work all day. She hoed the weeds, she stripped the cobs, she milked the cows, she stirred the putu. But when Sun sank low in the west and the evening breeze came to cool the hot earth she would grow strangely restless. Sometimes she would look up suddenly as if she had heard someone call. I did everything I could to make her happy and contented. I made her pretty bead anklets and plaited the coloured grasses into bracelets for her wrists. I played games with her and told her stories. But somehow I knew I was going to lose her.

Then one evening as we were going to milk the cows Wind rose, blowing strongly from the east towards the mountains. Moya stood still for a moment, her head slightly tilted, listening. Her eyes began to sparkle. She ran across to the old brown cow and put her arms about its neck. I followed quietly with a great fear in my heart. "Tonight," I heard her say, "tonight I must go. Come give me your milk for the last time." I knew

that the cow was old and had long been dry but as Moya began to squeeze the udders the rich yellow milk shot forth in great spurts and soon she had filled many gourds — more than you have fingers on both hands — and still the milk flowed.

She brought the gourds to me to set under the trees for making amasi and I saw her hands were trembling with excitement. "Little mother," she said, "I must leave you. My Great Mother calls. I must go home."

She stretched her arms up to the sky, to the wind-driven clouds that were now scudding across Moon. Then she began to dance, as lightly as a leaf on a tree in the evening breeze, and dancing she made her way to that knoll.

I had always been afraid of that place for the pool under those trees, though small, is very deep and cold and still. Besides, loquat and baobab grow there side by side, and nowhere else do they grow together, nowhere. There was always something I did not understand about that place, always something fearful. But I followed her.

The grass parted before Moya's feet — you can see the path still though we never use it. The weaver birds moved restlessly in their great nests as she passed. Widow Bird left off her preening. Bulbul forgot to call. As we made our way up the slope loquat and baobab, wait-a-minute and msasa parted their branches for her and willow drooped her head. The clouds covered Moon's face and the light of the stars danced on the pool as Wind ruffled the surface. "Manyeleti," cried Moya, "Manyeleti, place of stars, I come."

She turned towards me for a moment. "Good-bye, little mother," she said, "Good-bye."

Wind rose to a shrill cry. The clouds fled from Moon's face and she shone full and clear. The waters opened in a hole that whirled round and round.

Moya stepped into the pool and the waters closed over her. Wind fell silent. Moon hid behind the mountains. I was alone.'

First Woman sat very still. There was no sound in the air.

'It was a long time before you returned,' said First Man at last. 'I thought I had lost you too.'

'I had to come back,' First Woman said simply, 'I knew you would be waiting for your supper.'

12

APE

Vugiswe and his new wife had returned to the plains. Niame was young and strong, beautiful and good, and Vugiswe was well pleased with her. But Niame was very homesick for her people beyond the mountains. She had worked hard at building her new hut and First Woman had helped her thatch it well. It was a better home than she had ever had before but she longed for her own brothers and sisters, for her father and mother.

As she sat feeding the fire beneath her cooking pot her eyes filled with tears. Vugiswe saw. He took her hand.

'Come,' he said, 'sit close to me. You are tired, that is why you are lonely. You will learn to love the plains and foothills as I do and you will learn to love First Woman for she is truly a great and wonderful person. Listen, I will tell you one of her stories to make you laugh. I will tell you why Ape has no tail.

When the world was young Ape had a very long tail of which he was very proud. He and Hare were great friends. That was before Hare was cursed – but I will tell you that story another time. Ape loved to sit on the rocks in the warm sunshine while his wife combed his tail and picked the fleas off him, and Hare frolicked and turned somersaults to amuse him. Ape was very lazy but Hare was happy to bring him his food every day for Ape told funny stories to make Hare laugh and then laughed himself at the tales of his wickedness that Hare told in return.

One morning Ape woke in a very bad mood. Wind had blown hard all night and ruffled his hair and kept him awake. And his wife had obviously missed a flea on his tail the day before and it had run all over his body, making his skin itch and giving him bad dreams.

So when Hare appeared with two gourds of grain, one for himself and one for Ape, Ape snatched them both and shouted at Hare, "I'm hungry today. I'll eat *all* the grain. Now go away and let me sleep."

Hare crept away. Before Sun went down he was very hungry and very angry. He determined to play a trick on Ape.

The next morning Hare arrived as usual, carrying two large gourds, one of grain and one of fruit. On his head was balanced a calabash of milk. Ape could hardly believe his eyes. Hare had never before brought him so much food, or such good food. He ate greedily and did not even ask Hare to have so much as a bite. But Hare did not mind. He had made his plan.

"Ape, my friend," he said, when the meal was over and not a drop was

left, "Ape, my friend, I have found a field full of delicious maize. The grains are sweet and fat." Ape's mouth began to water. There was nothing he liked better than maize. "I tried to bring you some cobs," Hare went on, "but they are so big and so heavy that I cannot carry them. I can pick them for you and lay them in a large pile, but I cannot carry them for I am only a small weak creature. You are a big strong animal. You could carry them. I will go down to the field this evening and pick the cobs and you come down, when Moon has risen, and collect them."

Ape being lazy did not really want to collect the maize himself, but being greedy he could not resist the idea of such a feast and he agreed to meet Hare in the maize field when Moon stood exactly above the wait-a-minute tree.

Meanwhile Hare slipped like a shadow over the rocks, through the long grass towards First Woman's maize field. There he sat down and laughed until he thought his sides would burst.

He called to his wife. "Wife," he said, "I wish to plait a long and very strong rope. Call all our children together to cut as much long grass as you can find and bring it to me."

Hare's wife and children cut grass all day and Hare plaited a long, thick, strong rope, one end of which he tied tightly to the trunk of the wait-a-minute tree. He stretched the rest of the rope through the grass to First Woman's maize field. Waiting until First Woman went out to milk the cows he picked several large cobs and placed them in a little pile near the rope end. He sat down to wait.

Coming back from her milking First Woman saw Hare sitting still and quietly in her field. Normally she would have thrown a stone at him and chased him away for Hare is an evil creature, but she was carrying two gourds of milk in her hands as well as one on her head so she let him be and went on into the hut to prepare the supper.

Moon rose in the east and Hare watched her ride across the sky. She now stood right over the wait-a-minute tree. He tugged at the rope. Yes, it was made fast. He waited. A pebble clattered lightly over the grey rocks. Ape was coming.

Hare laid a paw on his whisker to show Ape that he must be very quiet, then beckoned to him.

"Shh, make no noise Ape," he whispered. "First Man has returned and they are all busy eating in the hut. See, here are the cobs. Pick them up and I will climb up and throw you down some more."

Ape bent over to gather the cobs. His beautiful bushy tail gleamed silvery grey in the moonlight. Very quietly Hare slipped the rope round the tail and tied it tight. Then he somersaulted over to First Woman's hut, beat with his paws on the walls and shouted, "First Woman, First Woman, someone is stealing your maize."

45

Out came, not First Woman but First Man, carrying a small branch. Ape backed from him in terror and tried to run but the rope round his tail held him fast.

"Take that, and that, and that," shouted First Man, beating Ape about his head, his back, his haunches.

Ape heaved and strained, and strained and heaved to try to escape the dreadful blows, until, quite suddenly, his tail came off and turning head over heels he found himself free to scamper back to his worried wife who had heard the shouting and the barking and the grunting and had been wondering whatever could be happening.

"I have brought you some maize," panted Ape, "and ..."

But he got no further. Round him in a circle sat all his children, laughing and chattering at the extraordinary sight of Ape's bare bottom — for his tail was still tied to the wait-a-minute tree.

From that day on Ape's children have had no tails; and Hare has never dared visit Ape again.'

Niame laughed and clapped her hands.

'Aaow,' she said, 'and what became of the tail?'

'First Woman made it into a fur hat for First Man. He wears it when Wind blows cold,' said Vugiswe. 'Come, you are happy now. Let us go to sleep.'

13

NDHLOVU

First Woman was busy making tiny little squares of seed pods and beads, *really* tiny squares. She would join them together this evening into a tiny necklace. She had already made some anklets and bracelets, very, very small ones, and had cured and softened a monkey skin to make a warm, furry blanket. Tonight Niame would have her first baby.

Great care was being taken to protect the new child. Niame would come to First Woman's hut and have the baby there. This meant that First Woman could guard her.

First Woman had stuffed all the cracks and spaces between the thatch and walls with grass and mud so that Wind could not enter nor Moon shine through. She remembered Moya and did not want Niame's child to seek Manyeleti.

She had milked the cows early and set plenty of milk in the gourds under the trees but had kept a great calabash full of fresh, foaming, creamy milk for Niame herself.

And First Woman had invited Tokoloshi. She did not actually speak to him, for one seldom sees Tokoloshi, but she spoke to the grass which whispered her message across the plains, and to the trees who fluttered her message into the air. She told Bulbul and Widow-bird who would chirp the news far and wide; and River who would carry the invitation right down to Sea, just in case Tokoloshi should be there. She set a large calabash of cream just outside the hut door, for there is nothing that Tokoloshi loves better than cream, and First Man had slaughtered a young bullock so that she could make a delicious stew which Tokoloshi would be sure to smell. Oh yes, she knew Tokoloshi would be there.

First Man came in.

'Are your necklaces finished?' he said.

'Yes,' answered First Woman. 'See, I have made two. This pattern is for a boy-baby and this,' she drew one from under the monkey skin, 'is for a girl-baby. I hope Niame has a girl-baby.' First Woman glanced round the hut to make extra certain there was nowhere Wind could enter. 'She could help me in the fields when she is older and when she grows up she will bring a good bride price to Vugiswe.'

But First Man was thinking of Moya, his girl-child, and he shivered a little. 'No, I want a boy-child for her,' he said. 'It is better her first child be a boy. Vugiswe would like that. Later she can have girl-babies.'

First Woman sighed. 'Yes, perhaps that would be better.'

Just then a feather seemed to touch First Woman's cheek and she knew Tokoloshi had come. She must tell Niame about Tokoloshi.

'What will they call the boy-baby?' she asked First Man.

Before he could answer Niame arrived and they hurried her into the hut, hanging antelope skins across the doorway to keep out Moon and Wind.

The night was very quiet. First Man and Vugiswe sat outside, beside Fire. First Woman and Tokoloshi stayed with Niame.

Suddenly there was a cry from within, a good strong, wailing cry. First Man smiled. 'Such a strong cry,' he said. 'It is surely a boy-baby.' Vugiswe went swiftly inside, noticing, as he did so, that Tokoloshi had drunk all the cream from the calabash. He took his son from Niame's arms.

'So,' he said, 'a fine, healthy boy-baby. We shall call him Ndhlovu.'

'Ndhlovu? The Elephant?' asked Niame in amazement.

'Yes,' answered Vugiswe. 'Ndhlovu the Elephant. When you have fed the baby and wrapped him in his monkey skin I will tell you the story of First Woman and Elephant and you will understand.'

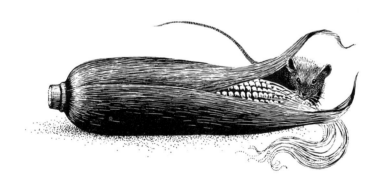

14

FIRST WOMAN AND ELEPHANT

When Niame had fed her baby in the morning and wrapped him in his monkey skin blanket she took him into the sun with her where she could sit with Vugiswe and hear the story of First Woman and Elephant.

'When First Woman and First Man first rose from the pool,' began Vugiswe, 'they had to beware of Elephant for when the world was new Elephant, like Lion, loved the taste of man's flesh.

When my sister Moya, the child of the winds, was very young, First Woman used to leave Fire burning outside the hut all day while she worked in the fields so that neither Elephant nor Lion would dare approach the child as she played.

But Moya was a wayward child, often disobedient, and one day, when the winds were blowing across the plain, Moya left the hut and wandered down to River. Drinking there and spraying himself with the cool water was Elephant. He was hungry and irritable and he did not hesitate to pick Moya up in his trunk, whirl her once through the air, put her in his mouth and swallow her.

First Woman, returning to the hut, found her child gone and great was her sorrow. She searched around the deep pool; she searched along River's banks; she searched in the long grass; she searched until she was sick with fatigue and worry. Just as she was about to set out for the sacred pool — yes, she was willing to visit even that dreadful place although it had not yet become Moya's home — Tokoloshi brushed against her cheek and whispered "Elephant". She knew then, with terrible certainty, that Elephant had eaten her child. She also knew what she must do.

Taking up the small scythe she used for cutting thatching-grass, she hid it under her skirt and set off across the plain.

With a flash of red Bee-eater descended on Kori-Bustard's back.

"Bee-eater, little Bee-eater," said First Woman, "Elephant has taken my child and I cannot find him anywhere."

"He has gone past the lake on the knoll and is even now following River towards the foothills," chirped Bee-eater.

First Woman went past the knoll and down to River. Here she found Fish.

"Fish, contented Fish," she said, "Elephant has taken my child and I cannot find him anywhere."

"He has drunk from River and crossed over the large foot stones and is

making his way to the kranz where Scorpion lives," gasped Fish.

First Woman crossed the foot stones and went on to the kranz where Scorpion lives. There she met Kori-Bustard.

"Kori-kori," she said, "slayer of Scorpion. Elephant has taken my child and I cannot find him anywhere."

"He has passed by the kranz and is even now among the trees covering the foothills of the great mountains," cawed Kori-Bustard.

First Woman made her way to the foothills. When she reached the edge of the belt of trees she saw Fly-catcher.

"Fly-catcher, you of the long crimson tail," she said, "Elephant has taken my child and I cannot find him anywhere."

"Sshhh, First Woman," trilled Fly-catcher very softly, "Elephant is here sleeping under the duni-gum trees. Sssshhhhh."

First Woman crept forward and there, sure enough, was Elephant's great grey bulk. She trembled. She feared Elephant greatly but she knew what she must do if she were to save her child. She stood up straight.

"Elephant," she said loudly and rudely, "big, fat, greedy Elephant, give me back my child or I shall strike you across the tip of your trunk until your eyes water."

Elephant opened one button eye, then the other. He yawned, stretched out his trunk, picked up First Woman, popped her into his mouth and swallowed her. This was exactly what First Woman had hoped for.

Inside the huge cave that was Elephant's stomach, it was very dark. She stood still while her eyes grew used to this grey-black light. Then she saw Moya crouched in terror against Elephant's side.

"Hush you," she said softly, and opened her arms. "Hush you. First Woman is here to save you." She cradled Moya in her arms. "Lie still until Elephant sleeps again."

Soon the rumbling of Elephant's snores reached First Woman's ears and she knew she must work quickly now before the great animal woke again.

Taking the scythe from under her skirt she started cutting through Elephant's stomach. Back and forth went the scythe, up and down, until there was a hole large enough for First Woman and Moya to step out into the fresh air.

With some thorns from the wait-a-minute tree First Woman carefully and neatly closed up the hole they had made and picking up her daughter she hurried off out of the belt of trees, past the kranz where Scorpion lives, over the foot stones, past the knoll of the sacred lake, along River's banks and back to the safety of the hut.

Elephant woke with a great pain in his side. He trumpeted until the mountains themselves shook with the noise but he knew that First Woman had been victorious.

Since then, while Elephant has remained the biggest and most powerful of all the beasts, he has never again hunted man, or stolen man's children, or eaten man's oxen. Of all the big animals he is the gentlest. He will trample all that is bad or cruel – he has even been known to trample Lion – but he never attacks First Woman's children.'

Niame looked down at the baby. 'Yes, you will be my baby Elephant, my Ndhlovu. You will grow big and powerful and trample all that is bad or cruel but you will remain gentle towards First Woman's children and her children's children.' She kissed the child's head and rocked him in her arms.

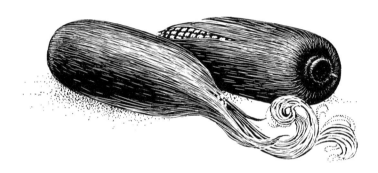

HYENA

First Woman and Niame were busy in the fields. First Woman was growing older and Niame often helped her after she had weeded her own maize. Ndhlovu was tied comfortably and safely on her back where he could sleep while she worked. In this way she need not leave him alone when she was busy. It was true Elephant would not touch him but there was always Lion or Jackal – and Wind. She had heard the story of Moya and she did not wish Ndhlovu to follow the winds to Manyeleti.

Although Sun had sunk very near the mountain tops it was still hot and First Woman, pausing to stretch her back and shoulders, was glad when Niame pointed out it was time Ndhlovu had his drink of milk – he always drank it out of Tokoloshi's calabash. They made their way back to the hut and sat down, their backs against the wall, their legs crossed.

Niame screwed up her nose. She could smell something unclean. She sniffed again then leaped to her feet. 'Hyena,' she cried and began running towards the pastures where the cows, with their young calves, were grazing.

'Hyena,' shouted First Woman, forgetting how tired she was. She too leaped up, grabbed her hoe and rushed after Niame.

The cows had formed a circle round their calves, facing out towards Hyena, their heads lowered, their horns ready to rip Hyena to pieces if he should attack their young.

Hyena dribbled. His spotted coat was rough and crusted with mud. He smelled. Of all animals only Hyena smells of stale dung. He made a rush at the cows and, dodging a long pointed horn, snapped at a leg to try to force the cows to break their circle and let him in. He fancied a nice fat calf for supper.

First Woman rushed at him, brandishing her hoe. Niame came at him from the opposite direction, waving her arms. The cows' horns poked at him. With a yelp Hyena turned and fled. Niame and First Woman made their way back to the hut.

'It is as well that you smelled Hyena,' said First Woman.

'Yes,' answered Niame, still a little breathless, 'he has a strong smell, the smell of stale dung.'

'Do you know why he smells that way?' asked First Woman.

Niame sat Ndhlovu down on his monkey-skin blanket, crossed her ankles, leaned back against the hut wall, and waited for the story she knew would come.

'When Nkulunkulu first made Hyena he gave him a smooth, shining coat like Dog's and he was a clean animal, though never a brave one. He has always followed Lion and eaten what Lion left, or attacked only small creatures like the baby calves. No, he has never been brave, but he was clean and sleek.

Then he made the mistake of choosing Hare for a friend. Everyone knew Hare was wicked. Hyena knew too but he thought he was clever enough to outwit Hare.

Hare and Hyena had been lolloping and somersaulting and leaping and rolling about in the grass all day and when evening came they were both hungry.

"I know where there is some excellent, juicy maize to be had," said Hare. "I will go for it while you prepare a glowing fire to roast the cobs."

When Hare returned, Hyena noticed with dismay that there were only as many cobs as he had toes on one paw and he knew this would not make supper for two. He would have to make a plan.

Hare put the cobs in the embers and the two animals sat watching the grains grow golden-brown. Hyena smiled a cunning smile to himself.

"I am just going down to the stream to fetch some water," he said. "Maize always makes me thirsty." He picked up a calabash shell. Hare watched him saunter away in to the dusk and frowned. Hyena usually sent *him* to fetch and carry. What was he up to now?

Hyena crept behind a loquat tree and quietly took off his skin. How dreadful he looked dressed only in his meat, his eyes glaring in the darkness, as he made his way back to Hare.

"Yaowoooooooooo," howled Hyena.

Hare leaped up, saw the hideous monster approaching and fled into the darkness. Hyena sat down and started to eat the maize, chuckling to himself.

Now when Hare had rushed off he had run straight to the loquat tree for its leaves were thick and its roots gnarled and he knew he would find a hiding place there. As he crouched down, his heart thumping with terror, what should he see but Hyena's skin? So! If Hyena's skin was here beneath the tree it was not on Hyena. The dreadful monster who had chased him off just a moment ago had not been wearing a skin either. Hyena would now be eating all the maize and laughing to think how easily he had tricked Hare. So!

Hare crept out from between the roots and carefully took down the skin. Quietly, and with a wicked smile on his face, and his split nose wrinkling with delight, he picked up two large pats of dung which the cows had dropped on their way to River. He rubbed them carefully over the *inside* of Hyena's skin. The dung was warm and fresh. It stuck in lumps here and there, in the shoulders, in the knees, round the ankles, behind the

ears, and as the dung dried the lumps became hard and crusty.

Hare put the skin back where he had found it and sauntered back towards the embers keeping in the shadow so that Hyena should not see him. Then, in a loud voice, he called out, "The monster is here, O Lion, O Leopard, O Elephant. Kill him for me, I beg you, for I fear him greatly."

Hyena shot to his feet. Lion! Leopard! Elephant! Had Hare in his great fear brought in these most dreaded animals to help hunt the "monster"? Hyena peered through the darkness but could see nothing.

"Do not tear me to pieces, Great Lion, Great Leopard," he howled, "I am only Hyena."

Hare shouted again in the darkness, "Trample him Great Elephant. How can he be Hyena? How can this red, skinless monster be our old friend Hyena?"

Elephant trample him to death! Oh no. He must put on his skin at once, so that all the animals could recognise him. Silently – he is used to moving silently through the bush – Hyena slunk away to the loquat tree, took his skin off the branch where it was hanging and put it on.

His shoulders itched. Something rubbed his ankles, his knees. His ears twitched. Hyena quivered all over. This was terrible. He rolled over and over on the grass to try to scratch his back; he rubbed his ears against the tree trunk; he licked his elbows and ankles. It was no use; his skin felt as if it were full of coarse sand and the itching became worse.

Hyena rushed back to where he had last heard Hare.

"Hare, help me, help me. I am going mad with the itch," he barked, piteously.

Hare was sitting beside the dying embers. He sniffed as Hyena approached.

"Hyena," he said, "You smell like stale dung. Please do not come near me. You are putting me off my dinner." Taking some roast corn from the embers Hare loped off across the plains and disappeared.

Hyena has had a rough, knobbly skin ever since and the smell of dung has never left him.'

'It is a good thing it hasn't,' laughed Niame, 'or we should never have known he was at the calves.'

57

16

HONEY BIRD

The calves which Hyena had tried to take for his supper had grown up now. Some were young cows, ready to have their own calves, ready to give milk. Two were young bullocks; one would provide meat for the cooking pot, one would grow stronger and sleeker to take the place of Mbulindhlelu, the first bull that Tokoloshi had brought out of the caves. Mbulindhlelu, he-who-had-come-first, was old now and wanted only to graze and sleep.

Niame spent much of her time caring for her herd, and First Woman's too, for a good daughter always cares for her mother, and Niame had taken Moya's place as daughter to First Woman when she became Vugiswe's wife.

Niame was busy grinding the maize into coarse yellow meal, just as First Woman did, when she heard Honey Bird call, 'Hon-eee, hon-eee'. She put down the flat grinding stones and called across to First Woman, 'Honey Bird calls. Come.' The two women set off, Niame carrying two large gourds.

Honey Bird flitted to the row of three wait-a-minute trees, settled on a branch, called 'Hon-eee', and waited. Niame reached the tree first. Honey Bird flitted on to Weeping Willow and waited. 'Hon-eee' he called. First Woman caught up with him. She was carrying a smouldering log from her fire. Honey Bird swooped down on to the first of the msasa trees. 'Hon-eee', he called, and waited. Buzzing lazily round the tree was a swarm of wild bees.

Niame stood back from the tree. First Woman, when she had regained her breath, for it had been a long chase, approached the tree holding the smouldering log high above her head. The grey smoke curled up towards the bees' nest, swirling round in clouds, and the bees fled, for no wild bees can stand smoke.

Niame climbed the tree, took all but one honeycomb — you must always leave one comb or the bees will go away for ever — and carefully handed them down to First Woman.

Holding the combs over the gourds First Woman squeezed out the thick, yellow honey then put the combs down in the grass.

'Come little Honey Bird,' she said, 'here are your combs, full of delicious little grubs and see, I have left some honey in them too.'

She turned to Niame and they set off back to their huts, each carrying a

gourd of sweetness. Honey Bird fluttered down and began pecking greedily at the combs. He did not fear the returning bees.

'Why does Honey Bird call us, First Woman?' asked Niame. 'Why does he not take the combs for himself?'

'Well,' said First Woman, balancing the gourd delicately on her head – it is always so much easier to carry things on one's head for it leaves one's hands free – 'well, it is like this.

'Before First Man and I rose from the pool Honey Bird was here. He could always find the bees' nests but he could never take the combs from them. He is too small to lift them. Besides, if his feathers became too sticky he would not be able to fly. One day Honey Bird saw Ratel crouched under Weeping Willow on River's banks.'

'Ratel? The little badger?' asked Niame.

'Yes, the same,' answered First Woman. 'Ratel loves honey dearly. He is greedy for honey and his thick fur protects him from the stings of bees. But Ratel's small eyes never see the swarms of bees in the daylight. He sees best at night when his eyes are wide open but bees sleep at night and there are no swarms to guide him to their nest.

Honey Bird had an idea. A very sensible creature is Honey Bird.

"Ratel," she said, "I have eyes that find the honey nests. You have paws with which to take the combs and a long snout with which to eat the honey. You love honey but you do not care for the waxy combs. I do not eat honey but I love the grubs in the holes of wax. I will find the nests and call you. You will take the combs down and we shall share the feast together."

For many, many moons Ratel and Honey Bird hunted together. But Ratel is shy and when First Man and I came to live on the plains Ratel went away from River's banks and made his home underground in the foothills, deep underground lest First Man should find him.'

'So Honey Bird calls to you now,' said Niame, 'to take down the combs from the nests?'

'Yes,' answered First Woman.

'You said Honey Bird did not eat the honey,' said Niame, 'yet you left honey in the combs. Why?'

'For Ratel,' answered First Woman. 'Ratel loves honey. He will be there now that we have left, and his long tongue will be licking up the yellow sweetness, leaving the grubs for Honey Bird.'

'I, too, shall be licking up the yellow sweetness, soon,' laughed Niame, 'for I shall mix the honey with the putu this evening.'

'We shall all feast,' said First Woman, feeling the weight of the full gourd on her head.

17

SNAKE

Ndhlovu sat beside First Woman in the sunshine outside her hut. She was really old now. Her face was covered in little lines and creases and her black tightly curled hair had little flecks of grey in it. He knew that meant she was very old. But her brown eyes were still large and soft and bright.

He loved First Woman. He knew she was very brave for Vugiswe had told him about Crocodile and Elephant; he knew she was very wise for was it not First Woman who had enslaved Dog and turned him into a hunter and protector; he knew she was greatly blessed, for did not Tokoloshi sometimes sit on her shoulder; but most of all he knew that she told stories as no-one else, not even Niame, could ever tell them.

He was looking towards River when he saw the grass shiver slightly and a small, black snake slithered across the path. With the speed of Lightning First Woman picked up a stone and threw it, hard and fiercely at Snake, clucking her tongue in anger and disappointment as she missed and the black shape went on its slippery way.

'Why do you hate Snake so much, First Woman?' he asked.

'Snake brought death into the world,' said First Woman and Ndhlovu had never heard her speak so harshly before. His eyes grew wide.

'Tell me,' he whispered.

First Woman shook her head a little as if to chase away her hard thoughts. She took Ndhlovu's hand in hers and her eyes were once more soft.

'Yes,' she said, 'man does not love Snake, but it was not always so. Were not First Man and I once Serpents? When the world was new Snake was beautiful to look upon and the friend of man, the friend of all creatures, even the friend of Nkulunkulu.

As the world grew older Nkulunkulu decided that he had yet his greatest gift to give to man, the gift of everlasting life. As man grew older he must be able to renew his body so that he could live forever. To do this, man must be able to change his skin.

Nkulunkulu packed all the new skins into two great baskets which his wife Nbelingane had woven from the reeds that grow near the sacred pool. He gave the basket to Duiker, the fastest of all the antelope.

"Take these skins," said Nkulunkulu, "and deliver them with all speed to man. Do not rest on the way or let the basket out of your sight for it has taken me many seasons to weave these skins and there are no more to be had."

Duiker took the basket and set off. Across the dry sandy wastes far off to the south he bounded; across the lands where the little yellow hunters live; over the hills of thorn bush where the game is scarce; right up to those mountains and down this side to the foot hills. There he met Snake.

"What have you in those baskets?" asked Snake.

"New life for man," panted Duiker. "Nkulunkulu has chosen me to be his messenger, to deliver these skins that man may live forever."

"Forever?" mused Snake.

Duiker was by this time very tired and thirsty. His tongue felt thick in his mouth and his lips were covered in a fine foam.

"Why do you not drink?" asked Snake slyly, for he had decided that he would take the new life for himself and his children.

Duiker could hear River bubbling over the stones not so very far away.

"Take care of my baskets, little black snake," said Duiker, quite forgetting Nkulunkulu's command never to let them out of his sight. "Guard them carefully while I go down to River to drink."

Duiker stepped daintily over the rocky outcrops, through the trees and down to River. With a sigh of happiness he plunged his nose into the cool water and drank until he could drink no more. He stepped into the water to cool his hooves and stood a moment, getting his breath back and breathing in the cool evening air. He had come a long way but tomorrow would see the end of his journey.

Duiker had forgotten Crocodile. While he dipped his hooves into River and swooshed the water over his nose and ears a long knobbly grey log was floating closer and closer and closer until, with one snap, Crocodile had caught Duiker by the leg and was carrying him down to his home under the water.

When Sun rose next morning Nkulunkulu's anger knew no bounds. Long he searched for Snake, in the trees, under the rocks, even in River, even in Manyeleti, but Snake was nowhere to be found. He had burrowed a long, deep hole into the ground and far below, in the darkness, he and his children and his children's children were rejoicing over the new skins in the basket.'

First Woman was silent. Nothing stirred. Ndhlovu put out a finger and touched her cheek very gently.

'Is that why Snake can change his skin so often and leave his old one in the grass?' he asked.

'Yes,' sighed First Woman. Her voice sounded quiet and far away. 'Yes.' There was another long pause. Then she added, 'And that is why all men must die.'

She closed her eyes and sat very still against the wall of the hut, her head turned towards Manyeleti, a little smile about her mouth. As First Woman's spirit made its way along Moya's path Willow drooped her

63

head and the finches moved restlessly about their nest. Then a black shadow, as long as your pointing finger and as dark as a moonless night, fluttered silently from her shoulder and was lost among the shadows in the grass.